BICYCLE TOURING HOW-TO

What We Learned

TIM AND DEBBIE BISHOP

OPEN
ROAD
PRESS

Publisher's Note

This publication is designed to provide helpful information about the subject matter covered. It is sold with the understanding that the publisher is not engaged in rendering professional bicycle touring services. If expert assistance is required, the service of an appropriate professional should be sought. There is no guarantee that the web addresses found in the appendix will work as intended. Readers who utilize them do so at their own risk. The publisher and authors are making no endorsements or representations that products mentioned herein will meet the readers' requirements or expectations.

This print edition, published in 2019 as a service to readers, contains the content that was published in e-book form in 2013. The only changes to that content were made to convert an e-book with hyperlinks to a print format. The web addresses embedded in those hyperlinks appear in newly created Appendix B.

Copyright © 2013 by Timothy G. Bishop and Deborah L. Bishop

All photography contained herein copyright © Timothy G. Bishop and Deborah L. Bishop dba Open Road Press

All rights reserved

No portion of this book may be reproduced, stored in a retrieval system, or transmitted in any form or by any means—electronic, mechanical, photocopy, recording, scanning, or other—except for brief quotations in critical reviews or articles, without the prior written permission of the publisher.

Published in Thompson's Station, TN, USA by Open Road Press.
www.openroadpress.com
First Edition

Library of Congress Control Number: 2019902115
Print edition ISBN: 978-0-9856248-9-7
E-book ISBN: 978-0-9856248-1-1

CONTENTS

Chapter 1. Pushing Off 1

Chapter 2. What It Takes 3

Chapter 3. What to Take 9

Chapter 4. Packing 19

Chapter 5. Launching the Tour 23

Chapter 6. Daily Routine 29

Chapter 7. Safe and Secure 35

Chapter 8. Technology 47

Chapter 9. Coast-to-Coast Cost 53

Chapter 10. Get Started Now 57

Appendix A: What We Took 59

Appendix B: Web Resources 65

Acknowledgments 69

CHAPTER 1
Pushing Off

Many people fantasize about riding a bicycle on the open road to parts unknown, embarking on a carefree existence while leaving responsibility and boredom behind. Although certain aspects of that fantasy may be true, bicycle touring can soon feel like another full-time job. We left for the open road following our wedding in June 2010. We discovered life from a refreshing and refreshed perspective, but not without its daily challenges.

If you are looking for a description of the grandeur of our experience, you will not find it in these pages. Rather, this is a compilation of the "how-to" facets of our adventure. We are preserving herein what we learned in our first-ever long-distance bicycle tour for the benefit of those who are considering their own tour. Our tour began with seeds planted in each of our minds and hearts years ago, long before we even met. The arrival of our fantastic journey launched us into the great unknown of not only new geography, but also a new life in marriage.

If you are interested in learning more about our tour and enjoying our story, please consider reading our book *Two Are Better: Midlife Newlyweds Bicycle Coast to Coast*. In it, you will find not only an account of our exciting trip and the life-changing events that led up to it, but also some beautiful scenery captured in unforgettable photography. *Two Are Better* will challenge and inspire you to move more aggressively toward accomplishing your own goals and dreams.

Questions, comments, and feedback are always welcome at www.openroadpress.com. We will do our best to respond to all constructive comments and questions. In the meantime, we hope you enjoy and benefit from the following content of our own personal transcontinental on-the-job training.

CHAPTER 2

What It Takes

You may be surprised to learn that a coast-to-coast bicycle ride is well within the reach of just about anyone who possesses the desire and drive to accomplish it. The most significant determinant for success is a strong will to complete the journey. One also needs an available block of time (about two months in our case), some modest financial resources to acquire quality equipment and to fund food and lodging along the way, knowledgeable advisors, and certain intangibles that will allow the would-be cross-country cyclist to persevere.

Conditioning

A healthy body with reasonable conditioning helps, but we were surprised to learn that the training and conditioning aspects of long-distance biking are not as important as one might expect. We are health-conscious individuals, but we were far from top-notch biking shape at the beginning of our journey. Neither of us typically rides more than 2,000 miles a year. With extremely limited spring training due to saturated schedules, we resolved to embark on the journey anyway. It is a myth that you need to be in great shape to complete the expedition. It is not a myth that you will work yourself into great shape as you approach the final days of your journey!

Key Equipment

To learn what equipment would be required for a cross-country bicycle trip, we found resources through the Internet and Adventure Cycling Association, a nonprofit organization based in Missoula, Montana, that supports and promotes long-distance touring. We also consulted with others who had more knowledge and experience. The advice of bike mechanics, recreational outfitters, and cyclists who had already undertaken long-distance bicycle tours proved invaluable. We developed a list of required items and began to research and acquire the preferred brands.

Since we lived five hours apart, we usually met on weekends to continue planning and purchasing items. Located halfway between us in Freeport, Maine, was L.L. Bean. Since L.L. Bean is open twenty-four hours, we were there at all hours of the night, gleaning expertise from the specialists who worked in either the bike shop or the camping store. One of the requirements of a successful bicycle tour is a willingness to ask for help, both as you prepare and while on the road.

> *Panniers are bicycling luggage. They usually consist of two pairs of bags hung over racks mounted to the bicycle's frame and wheel forks in both the front and the rear.*

Although the following chapter provides more commentary on equipment needs, the procurement of certain equipment, like the bicycles and panniers, is foundational to a bicycle tour. Therefore, we will touch on our purchase decisions now. By far, the most important equipment decision was the choice of bicycle. We decided on the tried and true Trek 520® touring bicycle, which proved to be an excellent choice. The Trek 520® has been a touring staple since the early 1980s. Fully loaded, the bike handled beautifully and was durable enough to withstand the many miles we traveled, virtually without incident. Because of our short preparation timeline, we had only two or three training rides to acclimate to the bikes. We shipped the bicycles west in advance of our flight's arrival, which eliminated about ten days of otherwise available training time on the Treks.

WHAT IT TAKES

A touring bicycle needs certain adjustments before a coast-to-coast tour. Most important is the selection of the seat. Debbie purchased a Specialized® Lithia Gel saddle and fared quite well. Her best "seat adjustment," however, came on the road when we each purchased a better-fitting pair of cycling shorts. Although Tim's new shorts helped, he was never able to find an optimal solution and suffered from saddle sores throughout the trip. His seat choice was a Terry™ Liberator Y. Several advisors had recommended that we ride many miles with the bikes before embarking, with seat selection being a primary reason. Because Tim had insufficient time to try out the seat, he toted his road bike seat with him on the trip. He switched seats a couple of times, yet his rear end found little relief. Even so, a sore hind end was a small price to pay for the ride of a lifetime!

During the bicycle adjustment phase, there are other cyclist-specific considerations. Particularly as we age, we become susceptible to the negative effects of repetitive motion. Our unique physique or past injuries provide clues to potential problems. It is important to address these concerns up front—a coast-to-coast tour brings new meaning to repetitive motion. Failure to do so can result in a miserable tour.

Tim's adjustments took into account neck, ankle, and foot issues. The bike shop installed a short, high-rise stem on his bike and adjusted its handlebars, which put his body in a more upright position, relieving undue pressure on the neck vertebrae. He added special padding to his shoes. During the trip, Tim needed to adjust these pads periodically due to the constant chafing from miles of pedaling. Debbie has had chronic knee and foot problems. Her mechanic ran a computerized analysis of her riding posture to optimize her bike's setup. They installed a narrower set of handlebars to match her shoulder width. Seat height is also an important adjustment that can create or prevent knee problems and excess chafing. We suffered no ill effects from our past injuries, so we were very pleased with our bicycle setups.

We acquired shoes that used mountain-bike cleats, the standard for touring and more conducive for walking. Road-shoe cleats protrude from the bottom of the shoe, creating an awkward walking position with direct pressure on the ball of the foot and excessive stretching of the Achilles tendon. Although we already owned broken-in road shoes, they were too uncomfortable for a tour of this magnitude.

The selection of panniers was the most difficult equipment purchase decision. We were essentially buying them sight unseen based on reviews and extended conversations with an Internet vendor located in Colorado. One important product feature was that the panniers be waterproof. We also wanted highly visible, reflective material for safety reasons. We immediately leaned toward the Cadillac of pannier manufacturers, Ortlieb®.

> *Ortlieb®'s panniers come in the roller or packer style. The roller-style pannier rolls down and folds over, much like a paper bag. There are straps with clips that prevent the rolled portion from unraveling. The packer-style pannier cinches with a drawstring, like a bag of marbles, and is then covered with a fitted, protective, waterproof flap that clips to adjustable straps on the bottom portion of the pannier.*

It was difficult to assess how much storage capacity to purchase. Heeding some good advice from the vendor, we began packing our gear in paper bags. We simulated gear that we had not yet purchased with what we assumed were similarly sized objects. Once the paper bags were packed, we measured the cubic volume and compared this to the various sizes of the panniers. This exercise was far from exact, but did provide a useful frame of reference.

Expedited shipping allowed us to acquire the panniers for our training rides. We installed them and learned how to pack them, even as we continued to acquire their contents. We outfitted Debbie's bicycle with a set of red roller-style panniers. We bought two larger panniers for the back and a smaller set for the front. We purchased somewhat larger packer-style panniers in yellow for Tim's bike. We also purchased handlebar bags for both bikes, which provided ready access to frequently used items. We were very pleased with the pannier setup.

Intangibles

Certain other intangible factors support a great experience and a successful outcome. A healthy fear and respect for the elements make for sounder decisions. While it is helpful to anticipate and try to prevent unnecessary challenges and catastrophes, one also needs to understand that many circumstances are beyond one's control. It takes some flexibility and faith to move forward and trust that things will work out.

The company you keep on a long bicycle tour can make the experience one to relish for a lifetime or one you cannot wait to finish. Can you imagine the potential for finding people in a random group whose company you just do not enjoy? On a cross-country tour, you need consensus on travel plans. Some people like to stop at certain places; others do not. Some ride much slower than others. Some are more dependent on assistance. Personal habits and behaviors can be annoying when living in close quarters. Remember, you will be spending time around the clock with these people. How will these idiosyncrasies be reconciled amongst strangers? Some riding days are stressful enough depending upon weather conditions and terrain. Add in challenging interpersonal relationships and the value of the experience can come into question. Choose your riding partner(s) carefully. As for us, we could not have chosen better!

Unquestionably, the most important determinant to a fulfilling cycling trip across the country is motivation. If you get discouraged or give up easily, then think twice about a cross-country bicycle tour. If physical exertion wears on your psyche, you're probably not cross-country cycling material. You must find physical exercise energizing rather than draining—or at least be willing to work through the first two weeks to bring your body to a point that it looks forward to each day's ride rather than dreading it. Remember, you will be cycling many miles on consecutive days. Here are some questions to consider: Do you thrive on challenges? Are you successful in achieving reasonable goals? Are you easily intimidated? Will riding or camping in poor weather conditions make you quit? Can you tolerate pain, such as riding with a sore bottom? (There is high probability you will have one.) Are you uncomfortable riding through cities or depressed areas? (There is high probability you will need to.) Being honest with oneself up front while adopting a reasonable set of expectations will set the stage for a satisfying trip.

CHAPTER 3

What to Take

So, you would like to venture cross-country on a bicycle. What should you take? You can find very helpful checklists published on the Internet. Here is a narrative to help guide the process of selecting equipment.

Bicycling Equipment

First, what about the bicycle? Unless one enjoys physical discomfort and repairing wheels on a regular basis, a road bike is inappropriate for self-supported touring. Some people may consider a road bike if they plan to pull a trailer rather than using just panniers, but a properly adjusted touring bicycle should offer more comfort. And although trailers are becoming more popular, most people still tour with panniers. The following information assumes panniers are used. When selecting a bicycle, realize you will be traveling thousands of miles in a relatively short time. You will also be carrying more weight than you do on your thirty-mile recreational rides. You need a comfortable, durable bicycle to maximize your experience.

Factors to consider in selecting a touring bicycle:
- *frame durability and riding comfort*
- *body posture on the bike*
- *additional braze-ons for flexibility in mounting racks*
- *three water bottle cages*
- *wheels with high spoke counts and double-walled rims to support a heavy load over all types of road surfaces*

- *sturdy, puncture-resistant touring tires for a comfortable and safe ride*
- *length of wheel base to prevent heels from rubbing against panniers when pedaling*
- *drop handlebars to accommodate multiple hand positions while riding and, therefore, to deter hand numbness and tingling*
- *bar-end shifters, which are easier to adjust when miles away from professional bike mechanics*
- *durable running gear with proven reliability to prevent mechanical failures in remote areas*

Touring fenders, which minimize the splashing of water and road grit onto body parts and running gear, are another consideration. Fenders add some additional weight and may be complicated to attach and remove for shipping purposes or rack repairs. Extra padding under the handlebar wraps is a great idea. Hand numbness and tingling were common issues for us even with extra padding. Both fenders and padding can be added while en route.

Regardless of the bicycle selection, you will most likely need to purchase a higher-end saddle to minimize chafing and saddle sores. Replacing the stock saddle seems to be an accepted industry practice. Because everyone's body shape and pelvis are unique, no stock seat would suffice for all riders. The rawhide leather saddles manufactured by Brooks seem to get high acclaim from Internet commentary. However, the feedback indicates they have an extremely long break-in period (i.e., thousands of miles), so be aware of this before purchasing one. Unfortunately, you need to ride selected saddles in order to assess them. See how and if your bike shop will work with you on this aspect of equipping your bike before you commit to purchasing the bicycle from them.

Some bicycles will come with pedals; others may give you the option of selecting your own. Durable SPD clip-in pedals used on mountain bikes are the design of choice for the touring cyclist. These pedals are symmetric and therefore have clip-in capabilities on either the top or bottom of the pedal. This design makes clipping into the pedal much easier than with other road-style pedals. It also provides a backup should one of the clip-in devices fail. You will also need a special shoe cleat to fit this pedal. The shoes should be lightweight and comfortable for walking. Ideally, the cleat should be recessed on the shoe, providing more comfort when walking. You will likely do more walking on your adventure than you may suspect.

For some of the considerations in selecting panniers, see the previous chapter. Moving on to other equipment, you will need to carry some tools to maintain and repair your bicycle when you are not close to a bike shop. Some nifty "multi-tools" provide a variety of Allen wrenches and spoke wrenches, a screwdriver, a chain-repair tool, and other handy tools, all in one lightweight device. You should also consider another type of multi-tool like a Swiss Army knife, which is well suited for camping. You will need some chain lube and a dedicated rag to keep the running gear free of debris on a regular basis. A lightweight brush, like a toothbrush, can also help. Otherwise, your chain and sprockets will wear faster and your pedaling will meet with more resistance. Store the brush, rag, and lube inside a ziplock bag to prevent oil and grease from leaking inside the pannier.

A good bicycle pump is crucial. Some models fit right under the top tube for handy and quick access. Spare parts are as important as the tools. Carrying spare tubes is essential. We were conservative and carried more than two. For good mechanics, two may suffice, especially if you bring a patch kit and know how to use it. CO2 cartridges can act as good backup for your pump. We also brought an adapter that converts the Schrader valve configuration found on most service station air hoses to our bicycle tubes' Presta valve configuration. We carried a light-duty foldable tire in case we shredded one of our good ones in a remote area. By the way, do not be surprised if you need to replace tires in the middle of your trip. We had one fail after 2,000 miles.

> *Schrader valves predate Presta valves. Schrader valves are larger with an air-release pin in the middle. Presta valves must be unscrewed to allow air to flow, which helps prevent high-pressure tires from deflating unintentionally.*

A spare set of brake pads is also a good idea. The screws that hold your racks onto the bicycle will invariably loosen, so bring some spare screws, bolts, and nuts. Bring some bungee cords, which are handy for many applications, such as holding items onto your rear bicycle rack. You should also stow some spare spokes where they will not bend. Throw in a few plastic zip ties of varying lengths. These weigh next to nothing and are handy. Duct tape is a versatile fix-it tool limited only by your creativity. Electrical tape may also come in handy. Your bicycle's manual and some lightweight how-to guides may also be helpful for the mechanically challenged.

Good lights are important. See the related discussion in the chapter entitled "Safe and Secure."

Clothing

You will be bringing two sets of clothes, street and biking, although there will be some crossover between the two. Selection of appropriate clothing will accommodate a comfortable and fun coast-to-coast trip. Here are some guiding principles. Consider the range of temperature and amount of sunlight to which you will be exposed. Do not create redundancy in clothing, except to bring extra underwear, cycling shorts, cycling jerseys, and cycling socks. Choose cycling apparel with highly visible colors and reflective qualities. Strive for lightweight and compressible (i.e., packable) clothing. Remember, the lighter and more compact the load, the easier the cycling will be. Err on the side of bringing multiple layers as opposed to bringing heavy clothes for warmth. The layered approach provides more flexibility to accommodate a wider range of intraday temperatures. Avoid cotton undergarments, as they need too much laundering and do not wick moisture away from your body as well as some of today's new synthetics. Cotton also does not pack as well. Use loose and wicking briefs when off the bike. Zip-off pants that convert to shorts provide space-saving versatility.

> *Stuff sacks are synthetic, lightweight cloth bags that allow the cyclist to store, compress, and organize clothing and other soft items. They can be purchased at department stores or outfitters, and they come in a variety of colors, sizes, and waterproofing. They customarily cinch shut with a drawstring, or roll down and clip.*

The location of the route (both latitude and altitude) and the season of your trip will help you estimate the expected range of temperatures. Check weather websites to find the temperature ranges along the route you will be traveling. Your camping plans should also influence your selection of clothing. Camping exposes you to the elements in the cooler evening and dewier early morning hours. In fact, you could experience temperatures near freezing even in the summer! You will need warm apparel for both your upper body and your legs. Another helpful principle is to equip yourself with base layers of varying weights, erring on the side of lightweight layers. If need be, these can be worn in tandem to form a thicker and warmer shield from the cold. As temperatures rise, shedding one of your layers is an easy way to achieve the proper level of comfort. Arm and leg warmers cover the naked skin exposed by short sleeves and shorts, respectively, and can be removed on the fly when the temperature rises.

If you are cycling during summer, expect plenty of exposure to sun and heat. You will need lightweight and breathable biking apparel as well as effective sunscreen. Protection from the sun comes in two forms: clothing and lotion. Debbie found some relief from the heat by wearing a water-soaked bandanna around her neck. Long-sleeved cycling jerseys can protect your arms. Take sun protection seriously! A severe burn can bring discomfort and threaten to end your tour early.

Despite the incredible streak of dry weather that we experienced, with only one half-hour of rain over two months of riding, inevitably you will be exposed to either rain or the threat of rain. When it does rain, staying dry is difficult unless you seek shelter. Consequently, quality waterproof cycling gear is important. Even with this gear, you can still plan to get wet! Nothing is perfect when it rains. You will have a better chance of staying warm if you focus on that. Wearing the most breathable waterproof technology will help you stay drier on the inside and, therefore, warmer. Tim found out the hard way when wearing lower-quality rain gear that he got wetter from perspiration than from precipitation. Spend the extra money on top-of-line breathable rain gear, which can double as a windbreaker on cooler, dry days, eliminating the need for an additional jacket.

You will need a pair of street shoes for comfort when off the bike. Either sandals or lightweight, packable sneakers will suffice, but make sure they are comfortable and supportive. After many hours in bike shoes, your feet will thank you. High-quality, well-padded cycling gloves are important. Despite having extra padding on our handlebars and well-padded gloves, we experienced routine tingling and numbing in the fingers, as well as some periodic discomfort in the hands and wrists. You may also want an extra pair of gloves without finger cutouts to combat colder temperatures. You can wear these over your biking gloves while riding and use them during a cold evening or morning at the campsite. A wicking balaclava is lightweight and packable, and can provide an additional source of warmth while riding or camping. We each took one of these but did not use them due to hot weather and limited camping. Regardless, we would bring these on another trip.

Certain cycling outer apparel can double for use when off the bike. Tim had one such "overcoat," which essentially was a lightweight, wonderfully packable fleece. He used this "coat" exclusively off the bike and could supplement it with base layers for extra warmth, which he rarely needed. Although you may want some more appropriate apparel for more formal settings like restaurants, churches, or entertainment venues, you will soon realize that most people will understand why you are dressed as a cyclist or camper once they discover your mission. Don't let the anticipation of a few occasions among people who you will never see again dictate bringing additional clothes. Keep it simple—aim for versatile, dual-purpose clothing. Ultimately, no one will care. We wore cycling jerseys and shorts on a church visit and still received a warm welcome.

Toiletries

Cycling apparel worn next to the skin should be laundered every day to prevent body sores. Include antibacterial soap in your toiletries, which you can also use for laundry. Toiletries should target the basic needs for hygiene. The following items should be included: alcohol swabs for daily cleansing of areas of the skin susceptible to bacteria, nail clippers, small comb, collapsible toothbrush, small tube of toothpaste, an adequate supply of any prescription medications, and a small cache of aspirin, ibuprofen, and antacid pills. Some Bag Balm® or other form of chamois crème to relieve saddle sores should also be included. Those who plan much camping should consider soap versatile enough to clean the body, hair, clothes, and dishes.

Camping Gear

The type of camping gear you bring will depend upon how much you intend to camp as well as the temperature range and area through which you plan to travel. The basics of camping are a tent, sleeping bags and pads, a stove, and a few other items such as utensils, bowls, matches, disposable hand/foot warmers, and rope. You can acquire and replace food along the way.

In deciding what to take for camping gear, remember the guiding principles of keeping the load small and light and avoiding extraneous items. We purchased a small, extremely light, and easily assembled two-man tent. We also purchased lightweight and compressible sleeping bags with modest temperature ratings due to our plans for many motel stays and summertime travel. It was amazing how compact these bags became when packed into their stuff sacks. Sleeping pad technology has improved significantly in recent years. Your tent should be large enough to fit the expanded footprint of your portable beds along with other contents you would want in the tent. As newlyweds, we preferred the cozier tent model. A pillow is unnecessary because clothing strategically placed into a stuff sack provides comparable padding for the head, although some may beg to differ!

The Big Agnes Seedhouse SL2 in Idaho. SL stands for super light!

Some form of bug repellent is a must. We also carried a coach's whistle. Although we were unsure about campsite visits by bears and other wild animals, the whistle would give our camping neighbors notice that all was not well in Camp Bishop. It was psychological protection from the wild or false security. Take your pick!

Our stove, with its self-contained pot, color-coded thermometer, and flint to ignite the fuel, heated only liquids. A small canister of fuel was screwed into the bottom before using. Accompanied with freeze-dried packets of food, instant oatmeal, coffee, and cocoa, the portable boiler was a simple way to prepare warm food and beverages when other food was unavailable. Cleanup after meals was also easy and fast. In hindsight, this efficient food preparation was an even bigger benefit than we initially appreciated because the time demands associated with daily riding, bathing, laundering, trip planning, and blogging were more significant than we had realized. Our bike bottles doubled as cups. We had small, lightweight plastic bowls for the oatmeal. The freeze-dried meals could be eaten right out of their packet. We each had a "spork knife," a durable plastic three-in-one spoon-shaped utensil with prongs and a saw-tooth edge. The utility of the spork knife demonstrates that simplicity in life can be liberating.

In today's day and age, a discussion of equipment needs must include devices that leverage technology. The separate chapter entitled "Technology" describes how our technology enhanced our experience.

CHAPTER 4

Packing

With your bicycle and gear in hand, what's the next step? It would be ideal to try some practice runs and see how the bike feels with a load on it. After attaching the racks to the bike and seeing how the panniers fit, it is time to pack the panniers.

Bikes with loaded panniers on day one

Here are some guidelines on packing. Weight balance is important for a stable and well-handling ride. Therefore, each rear pannier, fully packed, should weigh approximately the same.

The same can be said for each front pannier. Weigh each of the packed panniers by standing on scales with them. Subtract your body weight from this reading. Adjust the loads until you are satisfied with the balance. This equivalent weight distribution will balance the bike from side to side. Although the front panniers are typically smaller than the rear panniers, they should be assigned some of the heavier, smaller items in order to balance the bike from front to back. The front panniers will usually be somewhat lighter, but should not be disproportionately so. For example, the rear panniers should not weigh three times what the front panniers weigh. We carried some heavy items in our front panniers, with some bulkier but lighter items, like sleeping bags, pads, and clothing, in the rear. Adequate weight in the front of the bike helped the handling. We also found that placing some of the larger, softer items in the rear provided some padding in the event the bike fell. Since the rear panniers are larger and protrude beyond the width of both the rider and the front panniers, they are usually in the line of fire if the bike upsets.

A balanced load in motion

The loads should also be compressed to maximize space and reduce the risk of load shifting while riding. Stuff sacks will facilitate both compression and organization. If you are traveling with another person, you should also consider appropriate weight distribution between the two bikes. For example, since Debbie is the lighter of the two of us, we lightened her load. Each of us carried a load more appropriate to our relative weight and strength. Debbie had somewhat smaller capacity panniers to begin with, and Tim carried some of the heavier items.

You will need efficient access to packed items. Just as a library has a system to enable readers to locate its books, bicycling luggage also needs some organization to avoid confusion and to preserve precious time. Use stuff sacks to compress like items into their own separate bundle, which becomes one unit when packed into the pannier. Mark the stuff sacks with a permanent marker to identify their contents.

We used stuff sacks that varied by color and by size. Once we acclimated to our system, we were able to locate specific items by knowing the pannier it was located in and the color and size of its stuff sack. Reading the labels quickly confirmed that we had the right sack without having to open it. We used transparent ziplock bags for uncompressible items. These clear bags allowed us to see their contents without unloading them.

To illustrate, we had two large green stuff sacks for Tim's clothes. At the bottom of these sacks were the less frequently used items. He also carried two smaller blue stuff sacks that contained toiletries. Inside of these toiletry stuff sacks were clear ziplock bags with like items (e.g., a shaving bag, a bag for Debbie's cosmetics, and a bag for tooth care). One of Tim's front panniers, dubbed the "techno bag," was primarily dedicated to technology and contained its own stuff sack carrying the same "techno bag" name. The netbook computer had its own padded case to provide additional protection. We packed the camping supplies nearer to the bottom of the panniers than items like clothes, toiletries, and the techno bag because we camped sparingly. Some items were awkward or large enough that we placed them into a pannier without using a stuff sack.

Bear in mind that bicycle luggage is typically vertical, meaning that items at the bottom of either a pannier or a stuff sack are inaccessible until the items above them are removed. A packing system that minimizes the unpacking and repacking process is best. It may take a few weeks of fumbling through stuff sacks to make appropriate adjustments to your system. Time is a valuable commodity on a bicycle tour. Efficient packing will help to maximize it.

The handlebar bags should contain items that you want ready access to. Candidates for inclusion are sunscreen, glasses, sunglasses, insect repellent, dog repellent, daily snacks, moist antibacterial towelettes, a camera, an MP3 player, a notepad, pens, a day's supply of distributable material like fundraising flyers or business cards containing your blog address, a waterproof bag for credit card receipts, and a flashlight. Our bar bags were designed for easy removal and toting, suggesting that valuable items could also be stowed in them. A separate tool bag attached to the seat post will facilitate quick repairs without the need to fish through the panniers.

You can find our complete packing configuration in the Appendix A. Appendix B includes web addresses for information on various products.

CHAPTER 5

Launching the Tour

As the start of our tour drew near, certain important logistics would keep us on track. We needed to figure out how we, as well as our bicycles, panniers, and other belongings, would arrive at the starting point of our journey. We purchased two one-way airline tickets to the closest major airport, located in Portland, Oregon. Since the Portland airport was seventy-nine miles away from the ceremonial launching pad of our trip, we needed transportation to the ocean. Because we lived near the Boston airport and Debbie was familiar with local transportation options, getting to the airport of departure was less of a concern. For any individuals considering a coast-to-coast ride, their starting points in relation to the locations of their homes will create unique challenges in landing at their origins with all gear and equipment in hand.

Flying over snow-capped mountains

Knowing someone near our starting point who would enjoy helping us begin our journey was an incredible blessing. Debbie's cousin, Jim Massey, and his wife, Karen, provided invaluable logistical and psychological support during the countdown of our leap into the unknown. Prospective tourists who do not have the advantage of supportive people located near their origin will need to rely on the help of a bike shop and other local services. A chamber of commerce might be a good first contact. You should communicate with these services well in advance of your arrival.

Given airline regulations, pricing for oversized baggage, and notoriously rough baggage-handling practices, we decided to ship our bicycles using ground freight. You may choose to ship your bicycle directly to a host or a bike shop in close proximity to your launch site. It would have been most disappointing to arrive on the West Coast, ready to dip our rear wheels in the Pacific Ocean, only to find that our bicycles had not yet arrived or had not been assembled. It would also have been frustrating to discover poor workmanship in the reassembly process after we pedaled away from those services. Since we were relying on a remote bike shop to reassemble our bicycles, we scheduled an appointment compatible with our travel schedule. Because of Jim's working relationship with the shop we chose, we were satisfied that they were reputable and qualified to provide whatever pre-tour services we needed.

We chose to have a bike shop near our home disassemble the bikes, pack them, and ship them to the remote bike shop. Most reputable shops have this expertise, which helps minimize the risk of damage to the bicycle before the long journey begins. The shipping bike shop should document any key settings, like seat height, and place these measurements into the box for the receiving bike shop's use during reassembly. The bicycle is the most critical piece of gear and must be in excellent running condition to maximize the enjoyment of the trip and help ensure arrival at the journey's end. We contacted the bike shop that packed and shipped the bicycles well in advance so they could reserve time in their schedule. We addressed all scheduling logistics weeks before our intended departure.

Panniers can be shipped separately or checked with the airline. We chose the latter since we needed some of the items in the panniers before reuniting with our bicycles. We had three options for anything sent to the starting point: carry them on the bike for thousands of miles, ship them home, or discard them. Old, dispensable luggage from the attic or the Goodwill store can be handy at this stage. We were able to find two such pieces at a Goodwill store. After removing some sewn-in dividers, the panniers fit perfectly. Since we had already weighed each pannier when packing, we knew whether the packed luggage would fall within the airline's weight limitations and could adjust the load to minimize overweight charges. Airline regulations may also prohibit certain items, like CO_2 cartridges and fuel for the stove. We purchased these items after the flight to avoid delays with airline security. Upon landing, we toted the tattered luggage to our bicycles, removed the panniers, and discarded the bags. Our bicycles then carried our belongings the rest of the way!

Depending upon how far the destination airport is from the starting point of one's bicycle tour, local transportation may be necessary. Prospective tourists should make sure that the company providing the transportation can handle bicycles with sizeable luggage. The transportation schedule must also fit one's timetable. Booking a motel room at the launch site will provide shelter the night before you embark and a fresh start in the morning.

With preparations well in hand, Debbie enjoys the Pacific

Accepting Jim's offer to transport us to the Pacific Ocean allowed us to set up the bikes, complete with loaded panniers, and make adjustments before bicycling on the first day. Once we arrived at our starting point, we were able to devote all of our attention to celebrating our departure from the Pacific Ocean, saying our good-byes, and beginning the journey.

Another logistical consideration was how to transport our bicycles and our belongings home at the end of the trip. Post-trip transportation home could require arrangements with bike shops, airlines, friends, and local transportation. Since the time to complete a coast-to-coast tour is dependent upon unknown variables, defining the specific date and time when a trip will end is difficult. Therefore, we postponed making specific arrangements until we could project a likely trip ending date. Nevertheless, it would be helpful for prospective bicycle tourists to provide advance notice to those who will help return them home.

We ordered maps well in advance of our trip to ensure their availability and timely arrival. The earlier the maps arrive, the more time one has to become familiar with their design as well as the intended route. Preparation is helpful even though much of the route planning occurs daily along the way. Adventure Cycling Association maps have a wealth of information that help in the planning stages of a trip. We wished that we'd had time before leaving to become more familiar with these helpful navigational aids.

There are also some financial considerations before embarking. Tourists who plan to use motels extensively should join some rewards programs to earn points on motel stays. Good rewards programs reduce the overall cost of the trip. Members of the American Automobile Association can enjoy discounts at motels as well as complimentary travel material and advice. We used some of their state road maps and regretted not having others. Tourists should bring reward cards and AAA cards on their trip.

Tourists should also carry a couple of credit cards and some blank checks. Separating these credit cards minimizes the likelihood that both will be misplaced or stolen at the same time. We contacted our credit card companies in advance to let them know we would be incurring charges all the way across the country within the next two months. Otherwise, their fraud-prevention departments might have questioned the legitimacy of geographically dispersed charges and tried to contact us. We also made some advanced payments on our accounts to avoid punitive card fees on unpaid balances as we incurred charges along our journey. If one prepays for some of the anticipated charges, it helps to explain this to the credit card company so that they do not refund your credit balance. And, finally, load your credit card company's phone number into your cell phone in case the card disappears. These credit card measures will help ensure ample and available credit while traversing the country, preventing some headaches that could detract from the experience.

In anticipation that we might pass into Canada, we brought a passport and a PASScard. A driver's license is a key piece of identification that helped us through security at the airport. We also drove a car while on the trip and may have needed the license to cash checks. A debit card linked to a bank account with some available funds provided ready cash at ATMs. We had cycling jerseys with secure and ample pocket space, so these cards were stored in a safe and accessible place.

Anyone planning a long-distance bicycle tour should make provision for bills that will come due during one's absence. If you live alone, make provisions with the post office to hold your mail or forward it to a temporary address. Check current postal regulations. Regardless, you will have quite a stack of mail when you return.

CHAPTER 6

Daily Routine

One of our pre-trip advisors said, "You can prepare, and prepare, and prepare some more, but you will never be completely ready for what you are about to undertake." How right he was! We had certain ideas and expectations about how a cross-country bicycle trip would work, but until we pushed down on the pedal at the Pacific Ocean, we were just fantasizing. We were anticipating the simple exercise of pedaling for hours accompanied by the gracious warmth of the sun and a gentle breeze across our faces. However, we soon faced certain daily tasks that took far more time and attention than we had imagined. We each began to feel like we had moved from one structured job in our East Coast lives to another one on the road, albeit a much more enjoyable one with great perks. Once on the road, we learned certain disciplines that became essential for us to enjoy our ride.

One of the more important disciplines, as unglamorous as it may sound, was daily hygiene. We realized just how important this was after a couple of weeks of riding. Each of us developed some uncomfortable saddle sores. Daily hygiene on the road entailed more than taking a shower and brushing one's teeth. More important was to keep one's groin area clean and dried out. After each day's ride, we would shower and dry. Then we would apply alcohol swabs to our groin areas to keep skin pores clear and the area dry. Somehow, we had not fantasized about this before marriage! We would follow up our cleansing process by wearing loose and breathable underwear to help ensure these areas stayed dry.

Daily, we laundered any biking clothes that were next to the skin. The laundering process usually entailed soaking and rinsing the shirt, shorts, bra, and socks with hot water and antibacterial soap. We cleaned our gloves less frequently. We would hang all laundered apparel to dry overnight. In the morning, we would tether them inside out to the rear bike rack or panniers to air out and bake in the sun. We carried at least two changes of this clothing to ensure we would always have a clean and dry set to wear. When available, we would launder our clothes in a commercial washer. We would often apply antibacterial chamois crème on our new change of bike shorts before putting them on in the morning. We are still unclear how effective these types of balms are. Although they may eliminate bacteria, they also moisturize an area of the skin that we were painstakingly trying to keep dry, introducing an agent that could clog the pores.

Camelbak® is a company that brands products under the same name for hydration of endurance athletes. Most often, the product referred to as a Camelbak® is a hydration system that provides an uninterrupted supply of fluids. It is usually worn on the back and consists of a harness, bladder (often with a seventy-ounce capacity), and tube with attached nipple, or "bite valve" as the company calls it, used for drawing the fluid.

We replenished the water and energy drink mixes each evening. We would fill and, if possible, refrigerate all six water bottles and the two Camelbak® bladders overnight. If a freezer were available, we would instead freeze the water bottles. Two or three of the water bottles might contain energy drink mix. In the morning, at either the motel or a convenience store, we would add ice to the Camelbak® bladders and any unfrozen water bottles. We used several well-insulated bottles, which were worth the investment. These bottles preserved ice longer than the cheaper models. The Camelbak® bladder, insulated by its carrying sleeve, offered longer staying power for ice and cold water than any water bottle. Periodically, the inside of the Camelbak® bladder required cleaning with special tablets and a custom brush to prevent microorganisms from contaminating the water.

Typical scene at an atypical shower stall!

Typically, Debbie handled the laundry and water duties, while Tim downloaded photos from the cameras, set up the electronic device chargers, recorded the daily mileage and other pertinent information in the trip log, and began writing the blog. The electronic duties could take several hours to complete. Tim would also address navigational concerns, such as understanding the following day's route, reviewing the weather forecast, and considering accommodation options for the following evening.

Replenishing fluids on a 97-degree day

We restocked the fluids several times during the day, usually at a convenience store fountain soda machine where we could easily dispense ice directly into our bottles and Camelbaks®. Without proper hydration, a cross-country cyclist is asking for trouble. We also carried and consumed energy bars, bananas, and other various energy-producing snacks.

Camping added a unique twist to the daily requirements. The routine was more challenging and time-consuming. We needed to unpack more items, as well as pitch the tent and inflate the mattresses. Naturally, this process needed to be reversed in the morning. Showering and laundering were not as convenient,

DAILY ROUTINE

although many campgrounds provide adequate facilities to accomplish these tasks. Food preparation usually became our responsibility rather than that of a local restaurant. Moreover, comfort was lacking, whether resulting from a cold shower, cramped space in a tent (although we liked the close quarters!), inadequate mattress padding, a cold and damp morning, or a poor night's sleep in eerie surroundings. Whether camping or staying in a motel, the daily routine always consisted of the repetitious task of unpacking and repacking the panniers.

Application of sunscreen was a normal practice in the morning and throughout the day. For two people coming from indoor employment, we underestimated the importance of sunscreen early in the trip, resulting in some sore skin for several days. We had too little appreciation that we would be exposed to a full day of sunlight, including those hours when the sun was most intense. Preventative measures will help the cyclist avoid unnecessary discomfort and, worse yet, a medical issue stemming from sunburn that could jeopardize the entire trip. With the right precautions, soaking up this much sun was glorious, good for both body and mind.

Bicycle maintenance required periodic attention. We soon learned that a bumpy ride could dislodge the tongue that secured the bottom portion of a pannier to its rack. Therefore, we needed to check and possibly readjust them multiple times each day. We also learned the hard way that rack bolts tend to loosen on a regular basis, which prompted us to check these bolts at least daily. Periodically, we also monitored the tire pressure and cleaned the chain and running gear. We were fortunate to avoid rain for most of the trip, which helped alleviate maintenance on the running gear.

Eating healthy was a critically important ongoing task. Food consumption needs to be increased on a bicycle tour to sustain energy and strength. If you review our bicycle computer's estimate of our calorie consumption the day we climbed through Lolo Pass, you will gain a better understanding of the requirements. Pizza was a common evening meal due to its balanced nutrition, quick and universal accessibility, and reasonable cost. We also ate our share of pasta. A good breakfast with plenty of caloric intake and juice consumption was important. Pancakes and oatmeal were helpful when available. We often ate at Subway® when we spotted one during mealtime. Their bread and wide array of nutritional food replenished our bodies' carbohydrate stores. And, of course, we needed to treat ourselves periodically to one of our favorite destinations, Dairy Queen®, which helped increase our caloric intake. What a great side benefit to our trip—we could never eat enough calories and there was never a concern about packing on extra pounds!

Replenishment: an endless exercise!

After a long day of biking, a healthy and timely supper often competed for time with the other chores. A good night's sleep was also very important to sustaining energy and good humor on the road. As you might imagine, with competing priorities, not the least of which was the lovemaking passion of newlyweds, sleep sometimes drew the short straw! However, once we closed our eyes, falling asleep was usually easy, especially in the comfort of a climate-controlled motel room.

Mastering these tasks made the focus of the trip—the actual riding and sightseeing—more enjoyable. After several weeks of repeating this daily routine, our bodies, and in particular our muscles, felt great.

CHAPTER 7

Safe and Secure

Two types of security must be considered on a cross-country bicycle trip. The first is personal safety, while the second is property loss.

Personal Safety

Selecting appropriate routes and exercising safety precautions are the best techniques to manage the risk to personal safety. On our trip, Adventure Cycling Association's maps did a commendable job of routing us through interesting areas and minimizing our exposure to major highways. Nevertheless, no route can avert all risk. Becoming aware of one's surroundings through research and asking local people for help can enhance personal safety. Our passages through eastern Montana, Cleveland, and Buffalo exemplified the benefit of soliciting and heeding good advice. Regarding travel through run-down urban neighborhoods, it is generally best to pass through them early in the day without tarrying.

As for road safety, diligence and caution are paramount. A rearview mirror is an invaluable tool to monitor traffic approaching from the rear. Various models mount on either the person or the bicycle. The advantage of mounting on the person, on either eyeglasses or the helmet, is that the rider can control the field of vision by simply turning his head. With the mirror mounted to the handlebar, the cyclist may inadvertently steer into traffic to gain better visibility in the mirror. Without a mirror, the cyclist cannot see behind him without turning his body. When looking behind, the body twists to the left. The rider will tend to steer the bicycle in the direction the body is turning, which reintroduces the possibility of steering into traffic.

 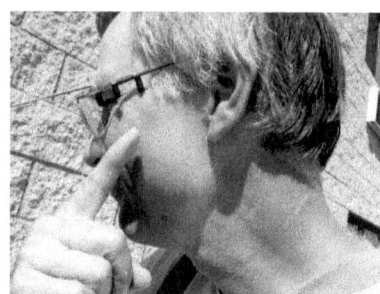

Rearview mirrors, whether helmet-mounted with duct tape or glasses-mounted, are vital for safety.

A bicycle is no match for a motorized vehicle. Both traffic and road conditions can pose high risk. Some roads are narrow, some have poor pavement, some have inadequate shoulders, and some have fast traffic. Other roads may have all four shortcomings. In certain parts of Montana, there was apparently no speed limit, as cars sped by at eighty or ninety miles per hour. We also noted little to no law enforcement on these stretches of road—only small white crosses on the roadside to commemorate another traffic fatality, reminding passersby of the dangers of high speed.

Respecting the space of motorists or more aggressively claiming space on narrow roads are both important safety techniques. Sometimes, as the saying goes, the best defense is a good offense. If sharing a dangerously narrow road with a car runs you the risk of getting pushed off its edge, then it is sometimes better to ride in the middle of the travel lane, blocking any slow-moving vehicle behind you until you are able to allow it to pass without risk to either of you. This more aggressive technique may annoy the motorist, inciting him or her to cause harm. Therefore, use good judgment. Every circumstance is unique.

SAFE AND SECURE

A grim reminder of high-speed fatalities

A long-distance bicycle tour invariably entails climbing and descending hills. If you stop on a steep incline, you may be asking for a long uphill walk. Loaded bicycles are not easy to balance. And it takes more power to start them on an incline. Therefore, think twice before stopping in the middle of a steep climb.

When beginning a descent, the extra weight on a touring bike accentuates the effect of gravity. Do not ride the bicycle faster than you are comfortable doing. Crashing at high speed is more likely and more risky. If it happens, you may just have ended your tour early. Maintaining control of the bicycle or stopping on a descent may be difficult if you are moving too fast. The grade on some descents is steeper at the bottom. If you are having trouble slowing the bike at, for example, a 10 percent grade, what happens when you are already moving fast and the grade increases to 14 percent? It is also more difficult to avoid unseen objects, wildlife, or roadway hazards at higher speeds.

Clip-in pedals can cause problems, particularly when starting and stopping a loaded bike. Unclip or clip in only when traffic is clear. Shift the bicycle into a less resistant gear before stopping. Turning radius is larger for a loaded touring bike than for your road or mountain bicycle. When slowing to make a U-turn in the middle of a roadway, you will need more of the road than you would on a lighter or smaller bicycle.

Road debris can often pose safety concerns. Constantly scan the road ahead to detect and prevent potential problems before they occur. Something as inconspicuous as a small piece of glass, a nail, or a wire can turn a delightful, seventy-five-mile day through a beautiful mountain pass into a discouraging, repair-shortened day.

If the wheel does not cross railroad tracks at a 90-degree angle, crossing the tracks can be hazardous because round, thin tires tend to slip on the metal rails and fall into the groove intended for the train wheels. When tracks cross the road at an angle, watch for traffic and then maneuver the bicycle to cross the tracks perpendicularly.

Wider roads sometimes come with rumble strips, which may or may not be bicycle-friendly. Rumble strips are systematic shallow cavities carved into the pavement to warn motorists who begin to drift off the travel lane. They are usually located between the travel lane and the breakdown lane. Some strips have breaks in them, allowing a bicyclist to cross them without traveling through the depressions in the strip. Rumble strips can effectively reduce the navigable width of the side of the road. During windy riding conditions with a heavy load, a cyclist needs a wider shoulder to maintain control of the bicycle. We had one day when this combination of road and wind conditions made traveling quite challenging.

Most traffic is respectful of bicycles with large loads. Others are simply unaware or careless. When vehicles approaching from the rear are simultaneously meeting traffic, the oncoming traffic poses the greatest risk to these approaching vehicles. Providing ample room for the bicycle becomes lower priority. Motorists will usually afford cyclists the space to the right of the white line.

If there is no stripe, drivers have lost a helpful guide and, therefore, cyclists need to exercise more caution. Some motorists will wait for the traffic to clear before passing cyclists. Most, however, will whiz by, leaving the cyclist with less room.

Recreational vehicles require a large footprint on the road. Their drivers, most of whom are not professionals, may be unaware of how wide their load is and where it lies in proximity to the road's shoulder. Whenever we saw these vehicles in our rearview mirrors, we were extra cautious to give them as much space as possible.

Rumble strip on Montana highway

Using Lights

It is definitely best to avoid riding after dark, but you will likely find yourself pedaling during twilight and after dark on multiple occasions as you stretch the day's journey to desirable accommodations for the evening. Appropriate lights that allow you to see where you are going after dark and allow motorists in both directions to see you are important. Using lights may lull you into a false sense of security. Even with lights, you will not be as visible to motorists as you would be in daylight. Cars pulling out of side roads have particular difficulty in seeing you because you are not in their headlight beams, and you may not even be in their field of vision. You should assume they do not see you unless they acknowledge you. When you are certain these motorists are yielding the right of way to you, proceed with caution. Otherwise, stop the bike and let them proceed.

Your field of view is particularly shorter, in fact very short, when riding at night. It is limited to the shorter of your light's beam, any ambient light, and your eye's ability to focus on distant, dimly lit objects. Road obstructions are more difficult to see at night. Use extreme caution. Slow down to compensate for the much shorter reaction time, and ride at a speed appropriate to your field of vision and your surroundings.

A headlamp strapped around your head or helmet can provide light for the road. Technology has improved these lights. They are easily adjustable and usually come with multiple lighting options. Do not skimp on either the beam options or the light's intensity—your safety is worth the extra money. Lights that attach to the handlebars can also be effective. The guidance about where to mount rearview mirrors pertains to front lights as well. A bike-mounted light may provide a more reliable indicator to motorists about your speed and direction than a head-mounted light. However, with a light mounted on the bike, the direction of the bicycle determines the cyclist's field of vision. The cyclist may be tempted to steer the bike to one side or the other to gain better lateral visibility. On the other hand, a head-mounted light allows the cyclist to see a larger radius simply by swiveling his head and to see longer distances simply by nodding.

Red taillights with a flashing option should be clipped onto your bike, panniers, helmet, or clothing. Make sure to use these wisely. Place them in a spot that will be conspicuous to trailing traffic regardless of your body position. Deploy them well before dark, as visibility diminishes quickly at dusk. Motorists will notice a flashing light more readily than a constant light. In addition, the flashing mode will maximize the battery life.

SAFE AND SECURE

Despite effective reflectors, Tim should have used lights here!

Head-mounted lamps are powerful and invaluable at a campsite as well, where wild animals may pose one of the most significant security risks. A neat campsite with all food and scented items stowed is one of the best defenses. Under no circumstances should you store food in your tent while you are in it. Some experts recommend suspending a food sack by attaching it to a rope and throwing the rope over the branch of a tree located some distance from the tent. The suspended food cache should clear enough distance from the branch, trunk, and ground to prevent a bear from reaching it. Campsites near the center of organized campgrounds can act as better cover as well. When camping alongside the road, check with local landowners who may be able to provide you with an acceptable parcel and some seclusion from the road. The wildest of creatures can sometimes be racing by in their vehicles at night!

Property Security

After traveling over 3,500 miles across the country, securing our bicycles and their contents is still an enigma. Property security is a trade-off between lugging additional weight versus minimizing the risk of property loss. It is also a trade-off between spending the time to lock devices versus gaining peace of mind. We carried a seven-foot plastic-covered cable with a heavy key-locking padlock. We used this system on only a handful of occasions. In hindsight, it may not have been worth carrying the extra weight. However, you may be glad you have one. It is impossible to predict whether you will need to leave the bicycles in the open, unattended, for an extended time.

During our trip, we often stayed at motel rooms where we could roll our bikes into the room. Storing the bicycles in the room was ideal because the bikes did not need to be unloaded, saving valuable time in the morning. There was little concern of someone stealing or vandalizing the bikes or their contents. And the security of the motel room gave us the freedom to explore by foot and relax for supper. When camping, the bikes were usually close to our tent. In a camping environment, you have limited control over who your neighbors are, so we sometimes locked the bikes. We placed valuables, like the computer, digital cameras, wallets, and cell phones, in the tent.

Awaiting the final day under cover of a Conway, NH, motel

SAFE AND SECURE

We also had a locking system for the panniers. Although the vendor was up front about the marginal value of this system, we decided to buy it anyway as the panniers alone cost about $900. The pannier locking system consisted of string-like cables threaded through a plastic rail on the back of each pannier. The exposed end of each cable was looped so it could be locked to adjacent cables or an external object with small padlocks. The installation was cumbersome. A modest set of wire cutters or a sharp knife could easily sever the cable. With no prior touring experience, we felt that the peace of mind was worth the minimal investment in the lightweight locking system. Since the panniers could be removed from the bike quickly without this security feature, the locking system was at least a deterrent. Of course, there was nothing to stop a thief from leaving the panniers on the bike while removing any of their contents.

The handlebar bag came with its own locking system, although a cable cutter could have removed the entire mount along with its bag. The cyclist could easily unlock the handlebar bag and carry it, along with its valuable contents, using its convenient shoulder strap. Nearly everything on the bike had unique value on a tour or it would not have made the trip. For example, one of the more valuable assets on the bike was the pump, attached via a frame mount. It was highly visible, readily accessible, and vulnerable to theft.

Our best security measure was to choose our stops wisely and to keep the bicycles and their cargo visible to us at all times. At one windowless bar where we stopped for lunch, the management allowed us to wheel our loaded bikes into the pool hall. When keeping the bikes in line of sight was not possible, we would take turns going outside to check on them. When stopping at stores and restaurants, we would usually park the bikes in front of a window and sit as close to the window as possible. This may sound obsessive, but when you are thousands of miles from home, it is uncomfortable to lose sight of your ticket home. At some point, you do realize that you are placing trust in your fellow man, whether you know him or not. Blind trust was easiest when we parked our bikes outside of church on a Sunday morning!

43

About to eat lunch with line of sight to our bicycles

Certain intangible factors work in favor of touring cyclists who are concerned about securing their bicycles. First, most people have an inherent respect for someone bicycling with such a large load. They assume you are on a long trip. We experienced this respect repeatedly, from friendly gestures, to warm and inquisitive conversations, to unsolicited offers of help and accommodations. Most people were supportive and understood our vulnerability. Many were delightfully envious. Assisting us allowed them to share in the excitement of our adventure. Second, because the bikes were heavy, somewhat awkward, and required special shoes, they were not easy to ride without some practice. A joyride would probably have been unsuccessful or unfulfilling. A potential thief would have had to plan his theft. The bikes required partial unloading to lift. Moreover, due to their size, they required a pickup truck to transport. Given these factors, it would have been more likely for a prankster to hide the bikes or for a derelict to vandalize them.

We lost two items to pilfer during our trip. One was a water bottle and the other was a loofah pad for scrubbing sensitive areas of the body. Maybe we simply lost this latter item from the bike, because who in their right mind would want it? Of course, they may not have been in their right mind.

Another type of loss can occur while on the road or at accommodations. Despite double inspections before leaving our accommodations, we inadvertently left some things behind. Tim left a new breathable shirt in the camp shower in Mayville, North Dakota. Sometimes, you simply slip up in your urgency to get rolling. Debbie lost one of her $100 sandals while riding in North Dakota. She was on a narrow, heavily traveled stretch of highway construction that made it difficult to conduct a prolonged search.

Laundry and other items carefully affixed, clear of running gear

Bungee cords, and how laundry and other items are affixed to the bicycle, pose another risk. Most of our possessions were like gold to us. But far worse than losing loosely attached items was the risk that they would dislodge, fall into the wheels or running gear, and damage the bicycle. Although invaluable, bungee cords that are either not well secured or wearing out can result in similar consequences.

CHAPTER 8

Technology

Today's technology can really enhance a coast-to-coast bicycle trip. Of course, today's technology becomes yesterday's technology as soon as this ink hits the blank page! Therefore, below is a general description of ways to use technology on a cross-country bicycle tour. The timing of our tour enabled us to take advantage of some of the benefits of both computer technology and wireless communications.

We carried a netbook computer. When choosing a computer, we focused on the bike-touring principle of keeping our load small and light. We wanted a good keyboard to support the daily content we anticipated posting to our blog. Good Internet connectivity and a long battery life were also important. The system of choice came with a wireless modem that would connect to free public wireless Internet access. In anticipation that public wireless Internet access might not always be available, we purchased a USB modem that would allow us to use cell phone communication towers to connect to the Internet. We then purchased two months of prepaid service with a wireless network provider to cover the expected duration of our trip. Most motels where we stayed had some form of free Internet service. We used the cell tower Internet technology when camping, at least in those areas that had access to cell towers. With ready access to the Internet and web-based e-mail, we could post blog updates almost daily. We could also check into the Internet's vast resources to find a local service, look up a telephone number, or order an item online and ship it to a forward destination. What an amazing world we live in today!

The netbook computer also acted as backup storage for photos downloaded from our digital cameras. Each of us took simple, point-and-shoot digital cameras, invaluable assets to document a trip of a lifetime. Tim carried his camera in a plastic baggie in one of his bike shirt's rear pockets, allowing for quick and ready access when the next inspiring sight appeared. Debbie's camera was at her disposal in her handlebar bag. Our computer could also charge these cameras with the same cable it used for downloading photos.

Connecting with the world

Our cameras also had video capabilities. In hindsight, we regret not having taken more videos to document our experience. We encountered some on-the-job training with the video art form. Our narratives needed a little work! Before we embarked on our trip, we did not understand the power and storage requirements of video shoots. We were also unsure of how to edit the videos and how they would work on the blog. We wish we'd had the time to experiment with this technology before venturing out. Cross-country cycling candidates should educate themselves on the art of producing videos. A separate video camera with editable video may enhance your experience.

A flexible tripod for the handlebars, accommodating an onboard video camera, would have added to the visual presentation and, ultimately, the memories. The viewer would have had a better feel for the on-bike experience, seeing both the traffic and the other biking partner in motion while hearing a narrative of the environs. Tim's nephew recommended this tripod during our preparation and procurement phase, but we rejected it, as other things seemed more important at the time. About two weeks into the trip, it became clearer how this tripod could have provided valuable footage of our experience. We were unable to locate one quickly over the next few weeks and chose not to order and drop ship it. It may be even more effective to affix the camera to the helmet or the body.

To let family and friends know where we were, how we were, and what we were experiencing, we wrote daily entries in a free Internet blog. Neither of us had had any experience with blogging before the trip. In fact, due to time constraints, we did not even select a blog site provider until we were on the road. If it were that difficult to learn how to maintain a blog, we would not have posted one. The blog site provider we used also allowed people who were reading the blog to post comments. It provided us with statistics on how many people were viewing our web pages and what pages or posts they were viewing the most. We subscribed to another free service that provided other information about the number of views on the blog. Knowing that so many people were following the blog and reading their timely comments were great sources of encouragement. We were also pleased we could share the joy of our experience with others. Downloading the photos and composing the blog required an hour or two of valuable time on a daily basis, but were well worth the investment. The blog and photography have become meaningful and lasting records of a truly glorious experience, captured in our book *Two Are Better: Midlife Newlyweds Bicycle Coast to Coast*.

We kept a computerized spreadsheet to track the daily and cumulative trip mileage, posting this information to a special "trip log" page of the blog, as we were able. Our blog followers quickly learned how to locate us each morning. We also kept a diary on the computer, representing a collection of drafts of the blog write-ups. We could complete a draft write-up offline, then connect to the Internet to copy and paste the daily blog text to the blog website. We would then upload selected photos and integrate them with the text to bring the day's blog entry to life. The files created and stored on the computer were periodically backed up to a flash drive in case something happened to the computer or files.

For navigation and record-keeping, Tim carried a bicycle-mounted GPS computer designed specifically for bicycle travel, a retirement gift from his previous employer. We regret having had insufficient time to explore the GPS's features more before embarking. For example, the device came with a full set of downloadable maps of North America. Without downloading these, we had a mere skeleton of what was available. And waypoint downloads from Adventure Cycling could have been installed into the GPS. The waypoints are essentially map coordinates drawing an entire route on the computer, helping to ensure we were always on track with Adventure Cycling's routes. The small size of the GPS computer facilitated easy removal from the bicycle and stowage in a bike shirt pocket when leaving the bicycle.

The GPS unit displayed elevation, speed, and distance as basic functions. It also had a cadence feature and heart-rate monitor. Again, due to our lack of preparation and ignorance of the features, we were unaware of how best to take advantage of this information. Upon returning, we learned that the trip information, including cadence and heart rate, could be uploaded to the Internet and shared with followers of the trip by linking the data right to our blog. This vendor-supported website provided a detailed map for each day of the entire trip. Each day's route could be "ridden" in simulation as well as linked to another website that provided aerial photographs of the locations we visited. We used the GPS to gather statistics and to determine direction when we were confused with the Adventure Cycling maps, an infrequent occurrence thanks to the reliability of the maps.

TECHNOLOGY

Debbie used a conventional bicycle speedometer for riding speed and trip distance. This speedometer would act as a backup device and crosscheck against the GPS computer. The GPS unit had battery limitations, which became an issue on long days or days when we were unable to charge the device fully before hitting the road.

We both carried cell phones. Our phones utilized separate networks, which helped maximize our coverage. Surprisingly, we did not use the cell phones frequently, reflecting just how busy we were. When on the Internet, we took advantage of our computer's built-in webcam with a free computer-to-computer communication technology that facilitated face-to-face conversations with family.

The cameras and the GPS computer required daily charging. Since we frequented motels, recharging the electronic devices became part of the daily post-trip routine. We also carried a portable electronic charger, one that itself could be charged (either from the wall or from long-term exposure to the sun), hold this charge, and dispense it on demand. We had some difficulty using this technology effectively. Thanks to the power readily available in motels, we did not need to understand the device better.

CHAPTER 9

Coast-to-Coast Cost

At the risk of publishing numbers that may soon become obsolete, we thought it might be helpful to share information about the cost of our cross-country bicycle tour. These figures presume that we had none of the requisite equipment beforehand. Any equipment already in hand reduced our total cash outlay. The total estimated cost of our trip was almost $19,000, as shown below.

Bicycles (2)	$2,800
Bicycle Parts, Accessories, and Repairs	1,200
Panniers	900
Camping Gear	1,400
Technology	1,700
Clothing	<u>2,300</u>
Subtotal Equipment	$10,300
Airfare (one-way only)	$800
Transporting Bicycles (two-way)	500
Maps	<u>200</u>
Subtotal Logistics	$1,500
Lodging (51 paid of 62 total nights)	$3,800
Food (63 total days)	<u>3,300</u>
Subtotal Room and Board	$7,100
Grand Total	$18,900

As you can see, equipment accounted for just over half of the total cost. And, as equipment, we will benefit from it in the future. Based on a sixty-three-day trip, the trip-specific costs (excluding equipment) were about $137 per day.

We were blessed to receive some gifts for the bike trip in celebration of Tim's retirement and our wedding. These consisted of gift cards at certain outfitters as well as certain pieces of equipment. As evidence of God's provision for our trip, we received some of these gifts even before we had decided to cycle across America!

There is an offsetting cash savings for any bicycle tourist. Simply by being on tour, the cyclist avoids certain other cash expenses, like weekly groceries and gasoline. A rough estimate of these costs for sixty-three days is about $2,000, or $32 per day. After all financial considerations, our net out-of-pocket cost for this trip was $14,000. Any future trips would come at much lower cost because we now own the necessary equipment.

There is truth to the adage "time is money." The slower you travel, the more days you will be on the road and away from your job, resulting in a higher cost to your trip. Some occupations, such as jobs in the education field, may allow you discretionary time in the summer, which is a prime time of year for touring. As a literacy specialist, Debbie was paid during the summer even though she had limited work obligations during that timeframe. With other occupations, however, obtaining a large block of time may be difficult and costly. For many, time away from work means no income. Pay lost due to taking time off for the trip is an additional cost not factored into the above analysis. Some jobs can be maintained while touring using mobile technology, preserving the tourist's primary source of income. Consider, however, that time devoted to work while on the road will detract from your adventure. At least for Debbie and me, we grew to appreciate that touring itself was a full-time job!

Can a crossing be accomplished for less than $19,000? Absolutely! Here are some ideas on how to trim costs. However, realize there were certain benefits associated with these costs, which is why we incurred them in the first place.

One significant cost saving measure is to camp more often to reduce motel charges. Camping is more time consuming and may compromise one's rest. Roughing it also poses risks that motel stays do not. However, for those who enjoy communing with nature, they can cut costs while increasing the adventure! Camping also may save money on meals, although many of our carbohydrate-loaded breakfasts were included in the cost of our motel stays.

Crossing in less than sixty-three days will also save money. Riding faster or longer in the day means devoting less time to enjoying the surroundings and adding more stress to your body.

Keeping the load light also adds cost. For example, our camping equipment was engineered to be light and, therefore, was expensive. A heavier load slows the rider and produces more strain on both the bicycle and the rider's body, either of which could break down. Tim carried a heavy load. His bicycle wheels fell slightly out of true, but Debbie's did not. Tim's bike also developed a rubbing noise that he was unable to diagnose and prevent. The bike's rear rack was prone to loosening and he burned through brake pads sooner than Debbie did. It is difficult to overemphasize the importance of keeping the load light.

Shipping the bicycles was more expensive than originally anticipated. Some alternative methods could save money. These alternatives are premised on the cyclist taking responsibility for the packing, unpacking, and assembly of the bikes. Make sure you have the necessary qualifications and materials before taking this on.

You can also tour with less technology. The higher-ticket items were the bicycle computer, the netbook computer with Internet cellular capabilities, a solar charger, and two digital cameras. For those who are less technical, simplifying by eliminating some of these devices may suit you well. However, remember that the trip will be over before you know it. There is underappreciated value in documenting a tour of this magnitude—at least until it is too late to capture the memories. Despite having more than 2,000 pictures, we wish we had taken more!

While on our trip, we experienced "stimulation overload." The pace of encounters with new places and people came faster than our minds and senses could process, although our brains stored these stimuli for future retrieval and appreciation. Many months after our trip, we debriefed our senses with the benefit of blog entries, photos, credit-card receipts, computer generated map routes, and conversations with one another. When the biking adventure becomes a distant memory, it will be difficult to summon unique memories from the recesses of the mind without the benefit of adequate memorabilia.

Our technology also offered an efficient way to keep family and friends abreast of our progress and experiences. Many found our blog to be a blessing, so we are glad we made the necessary investment of both time and money.

There are trade-offs between getting the most from the odyssey and saving money. When in doubt, someone considering such an adventure will not regret investing liberally. Paying up to minimize the load will maximize the experience. A comfortable mattress and a hot motel shower offer good payback. Unless one is mechanically astute, breaking down and reassembling one's bicycle may not be worth the hassle. A damaged bicycle will cost more than hiring others who are more proficient and experienced at packing them. Most people are not going to experience a tour like this more than once in a lifetime. A wholehearted devotion, including one's wallet, helps ensure a great experience. If you are considering a long-distance bicycle tour, make the once-in-a-lifetime adventure one that you can savor for a lifetime.

CHAPTER 10

Get Started Now

"No matter how much you prepare, you will never be totally prepared for what you are about to encounter." From our experience, those wise words from Danny, one of our pre-trip advisors, were right on the mark. If you are reading this material and thinking about taking the plunge, what are you waiting for? You are only getting older and reducing your odds that you will enjoy the open road from a bicycle seat. We encourage you to pursue your long-distance bicycle tour. And we hope this book has provided additional impetus toward that goal. You will never regret it.

You can learn more about our touring experience by reading our companion book *Two Are Better: Midlife Newlyweds Bicycle Coast to Coast*. *Two Are Better* is an inspirational story chronicling the events leading up to our tour and the tour itself, bringing to life the fears, passions, and vulnerabilities of two mid-lifers operating out of their element. The book is chock-full of beautiful photography from our journey.

We would love to hear from you at www.openroadpress.com. And please consider leaving a review on your favorite bookseller's website or on Goodreads to help other would-be bicycle tourists discover this book and begin their own journey. Thank you, and safe travels.

APPENDIX A

What We Took

Tim's bike

Trek 520® touring bicycle
Tubus® rack in front
Trek® stock rack in rear
4 Ortlieb® packer-style waterproof panniers and handlebar bag
Garmin Edge 705® bicycle computer mounted on stem
Topeak Road Morph® pump mounted under top tube
Rear rack with bungee cords:
> *Big Agnes Seedhouse SL2® tent*
> *2 used spare tires*

3 bottle racks for 20-ounce bottles:
> *1 unused when services available*
> *Usually 1 only with energy drink*
> *The other with water*

Debbie's bike

Trek 520® touring bicycle
Tubus® rack in front
Trek® stock rack in rear
4 Ortlieb® roller-style waterproof panniers and handlebar bag
Bontrager® bike speedometer mounted on top tube
Seat post toolbag:
> *Bike multi-tool*
> *Mini generic multi-tool*
> *First-aid kit, sewing kit, and patch kit*

Rear rack with bungee cords:
Clean laundry to dry

3 bottle racks for 20-ounce bottles:
2 with energy drinks
1 with water

On Tim

Helmet
Older glasses with mirror
Wicking sweatband when over 80 degrees, otherwise in bag
Biking gloves (sometimes, or in handlebar bag)
Up to 2 biking shorts depending on state of saddle sores
Biking socks
Biking shoes with two tongue pads each and right arch support
Biking shirt, pockets filled as follows:
Left rear pocket: camera in plastic baggie
Center rear pocket: cell phone in plastic baggie
Right rear pocket: mini lightweight nylon wallet containing:
Left pouch: cash, camera card, flash drive
Middle pouch: keys for pannier locks
Right pouch: credit/debit cards, PASScard, driver's license, AAA card, Choice Hotels® card, blank checks, receipts before transferring to receipt bag
Outside sleeves: business cards for bike shops or other resources

70 oz. Camelbak® for water with ice only

On Debbie

Helmet with mirror
Sunglasses
Bandanna
Biking gloves
Up to 2 biking shorts depending on state of saddle sores
Biking socks
Biking shoes
Bra
Biking shirt with rear pouch(es) containing:
Phone in baggie
Wallet with cash, cards, and keys

70 oz. Camelbak® for water with ice only

WHAT WE TOOK

In Tim's handlebar bag

    Glasses case with regular glasses
    2 backup Third Eye® mirrors for glasses
    Balm for rear end
    TheHopeLine™ card stock for immediate distribution
    Insect repellent
    Sunscreen stick
    Wind-up flashlight and small keychain flashlight
    Whistle
    Comb
    Up to 2 energy bars for the day
    Camera case
    MP3 player (not used or needed)
    Zip bag for credit-card receipts and backup credit card
    Pen, pencil, and notepad
    Map case with current bike map and road map

In Debbie's handlebar bag

    Wet Ones®
    Glasses case with regular glasses
    Insect repellent
    Up to 2 energy bars for the day
    Halt!™ dog repellent
    Toilet paper
    Garbage baggie
    Lip balm
    Bag balm® mini container
    Pen
    Sunscreen stick
    Camera with case
    Map case with devotional booklet and daily distributable TheHopeLine™ cards

In Tim's Left Front Pannier

    TheHopeLine™ flyers
    Jetboil® and backup fuel
    Sunscreen lotion
    Zip bag with antibacterial soap

2 blue small toiletries stuff sacks:
> *Zip baggie for teeth care items*
> *Spare bar soap or shampoos*
> *Zip baggies for Debbie's cosmetics, tweezers, magnifying mirror, grooming scissors, nail clippers, mini hairbrush, sleeping mask, earplugs*
> *Zip baggie for shaving gear*
> *Zip baggie for moisturizer, conditioner, shampoo*

Spare room for food

In Tim's Right Front Pannier

Netbook computer and power cord
Garmin® case with heart-rate monitor and charger
"Techno bag" stuff sack containing:
> *Solio® solar charger with power cable and tips for various devices*
> *Cell phone charge cables*
> *Camera charge cables and mini tripod*
> *Batteries*

Spare room for food

In Debbie's Left Front Pannier

Mountain House® camping food (usually 3 or 4)
Various levels of other food
Purchased items (minimal)
Biking journal
Energy drink mix
Camelbak® cleaning kit
Extra energy bars
Bag Balm®

In Debbie's Right Front Pannier

Journal
Souvenirs (minimal)
Peanut butter
Extra pair biking gloves
Spare bags
Sharpie®
Passport

WHAT WE TOOK

In Tim's Left Rear Pannier

Separate front pouch:
Used bike maps and state maps
Bike repair book
Trek 520® owner's manual
Spare spokes and bungee cords

Sneakers, with spare glasses and left arch support stuffed inside

Large green stuff sack #1 for clothing:
Polarfleece®
Midweight biking tights
Spare bike shorts (up to 2)
Biking shirts (1 long-sleeve, 1 short-sleeve)
Biking socks (3 pair, 1 wool)

Waterproof pants in individual sack

Waterproof jacket in individual sack

Small blue stuff sack for base layers:
Lycra® long johns (not used)
Medium-weight base layer shirt
Lightweight base layer shirt

Medium orange food sack #1:
Bowls and sporks
Oatmeal
Cocoa and instant breakfast mixes

Medium orange food sack #2:
Plastic coffee filter with teabag
Ramen noodles
Soup mix

In Tim's Right Rear Pannier

Separate front pouch:
Unused bike maps

Large green stuff sack #2 for clothing:
Underpants (2 wicking, 1 cotton)
Cotton socks (1)
North Face® wicking shirt
Convertible wicking pants/shorts
Cotton shorts (1)
Wicking plaid "dress shirt"
TheHopeLine™ shirt
Cloth belt
Hankie
Biking undershorts (1)

Therm-a-Rest® mattress in ziplock baggie

7-foot cable and padlock

Extra bike seat (not next time!)

Medium orange stuff sack for spare parts:
- *Duct tape and electrician's tape*
- *Nylon cord and zip ties*
- *Spare tubes (up to 5)*
- *Loctite®*
- *Spare brake pads*
- *Extra oil lube*
- *Separate bag for rag and oil lube*
- *Spare screws*
- *Presta/Schrader converting adapter*
- *CO2 cartridges (3)*
- *Patch kit*

In Debbie's Left Rear Pannier

Large green stuff sack #1 for clothes:
- *Up to 2 biking shorts*
- *2 short-sleeve biking shirts*
- *Arm warmers*
- *2 pair biking socks*
- *Medium-weight biking tights*
- *Bathing suit*
- *Medium-weight base layer shirt*

Large green stuff sack #2 for clothes:
- *3 short-sleeve street shirts*
- *1 long-sleeve street shirt*
- *1 wicking convertible pants*
- *1 street shorts*
- *Nightgown*
- *2 pair wicking underpants*
- *1 bra*
- *Belt*
- *TheHopeLine™ shirt*
- *2 cold-weather gloves (1 for Tim)*
- *2 balaclava (unused; 1 for Tim)*

Sandals

Rain jacket

Rain pants

Fleece jacket

In Debbie's Right Rear Pannier

2 Mountain Hardware Phantom 32® sleeping bags

Therm-a-Rest® camping pillow

Big Agnes® air mattress

2 camping towels and 1 washcloth

1 sleeping-bag liner

Interior pouch:
- *New Bontrager® spare tire*

APPENDIX B
Web Rources

The following list provides the complete addresses (URLs) to website links found in the e-book version of *Bicycle Touring How-To*.

Adventure Cycling Association (nonprofit bicycle touring advocate):
https://www.adventurecycling.org/

LL Bean (cycling equipment and outdoor gear):
https://www.llbean.com/

Trek 520 (touring bicycle):
https://www.trekbikes.com/us/en_US/bikes/adventure-touring-bikes/c/B250/

Ortlieb (panniers):
http://ortlieb.com/

Brooks (saddle):
https://www.brooksengland.com/

Allen wrench (definition and picture):
https://en.wikipedia.org/wiki/Hex_key

Spoke wrench (definition and picture):
https://en.wikipedia.org/wiki/Spoke_wrench

Swiss Army knife (definition and picture):
https://en.wikipedia.org/wiki/Swiss_Army_knife

Schrader valve (definition and picture):
https://en.wikipedia.org/wiki/Schrader_valve

Presta valve (definition and picture):
https://en.wikipedia.org/wiki/Presta_valve

Weather website:
https://weather.com/

Big Balm (body lubricant):
https://www.bagbalm.com/

Big Agnes (tent):
https://www.bigagnes.com/

Adventure Cycling Association (cycling maps):
https://www.adventurecycling.org/routes-and-maps/adventure-cycling-route-network/map-features/

American Automobile Association (road maps):
http://www.aaa.com/

US PassCard (border crossing ID card):
http://www.uspasscard.com/

Camelbak (hydration):
https://www.camelbak.com/

The Bishops' trip log:
http://bikersbishop.blogspot.com/p/trip-log.html

The Bishops' journal (trip blog):
http://bikersbishop.blogspot.com/

The Bishops' route map (trip map):
http://bikersbishop.blogspot.com/2011/09/interactive-map.html

Sample bicycle computer daily data dumps (Garmin Connect):
https://connect.garmin.com/modern/activity/48125703
https://connect.garmin.com/modern/activity/48125308
https://connect.garmin.com/modern/activity/48125601

Netbook computer (definition and picture):
https://en.wikipedia.org/wiki/Netbook

Verizon (USB modem):
https://www.verizonwireless.com/internet-devices/

WEB RESOURCES

Sample video (in-the-moment cycling clips):
http://bikersbishop.blogspot.com/2010/07/video-of-descent.html
http://bikersbishop.blogspot.com/2010/07/deb-descends-on-fort-benton.html

The Bishops' Youtube channel (edited and unedited cycling videos):
https://www.youtube.com/user/bikersbishop

Tachyon (small helmet-mountable video camera):
http://www.tachyoninc.com/

Google Blogger (DIY blog site):
https://www.blogger.com/

Sample comments on the Bishops' trip blog:
http://bikersbishop.blogspot.com/2010/08/bishop-bike-adventure-day-57-august-26.html?showComment=1282908702373%20-%20c2518020039686645167

Garmin (cycling computer):
https://buy.garmin.com/en-US/US/browse.ep?filters=cIntoSports+cCycling++

Adventure Cycling Association (electronic navigation):
https://www.adventurecycling.org/routes-and-maps/adventure-cycling-route-network/going-digital-app-or-gpx/

Skype (computer-to-computer video chat):
https://www.skype.com/en/

Goal Zero (portable power):
https://www.goalzero.com/

Tubus (bicycle racks):
https://www.tubus.com/

Topeak (Road Morph bicycle pump):
https://www.topeak.com/us/en/

Flash drive (definition and picture):
https://en.wikipedia.org/wiki/USB_flash_drive

Choice hotels (motel rewards program):
https://www.choicehotels.com/

Third Eye (bicycling mirrors):
https://www.3rd-eye.com/

TheHopeLine (nonprofit promoted by the Bishops on their tour):
https://www.thehopeline.com/

MP3 player (definition and picture):
https://en.wikipedia.org/wiki/MP3_player

Wet Ones (antibacterial hand wipes):
http://www.wetones.com/

Halt! (dog repellent):
http://www.halt.com/halt.html

Jet Boil (cooking stove):
https://www.jetboil.com/

Mountain House (freeze-dried meals):
https://www.mountainhouse.com/

Sharpie (permanent marking pens):
https://www.sharpie.com/

Lycra (long underwear):
https://www.lycra.com/en/

North Face (active apparel):
https://www.thenorthface.com/

Thermarest (lightweight air mattresses):
https://www.thermarest.com/

Loctite (cement to hold screws fast):
http://www.loctiteproducts.com/

Mountain Hardwear (lightweight sleeping bags):
https://www.mountainhardwear.com/

Maine Sport (outfitter who helped the Bishops launch their trip):
https://mainesport.com/

thetouringstore.com (vendor who helped the Bishops launch their trip):
https://thetouringstore.com/

ACKNOWLEDGMENTS

We have a full list of acknowledgments in our companion story, *Two Are Better: Midlife Newlyweds Bicycle Coast to Coast*, which chronicles our long-distance tour upon which this book is based. Nevertheless, we would like to express appreciation to our technical advisors from whom we gleaned much of the information shared in this book.

Danny Ricciotti, who bicycled coast to coast in 2009, was incredibly patient and helpful as someone nearly thirty years his senior barraged him with an extensive list of questions, from selection of gear to survival in the wild.

Glen Stairs is a cycling friend and gifted artisan who builds bicycles as a hobby. He willingly shared his unbiased insights as we acquired gear. He also helped on this book project by reviewing the technical material.

Matt Bishop, our nephew, who works in the recreational outfitter industry, was also very helpful in describing the attributes of clothing and camping gear alternatives. He also prepared a list of recommendations on camping gear.

Mike Hartley, who runs the bike shop at Maine Sport Outfitters in Rockport, Maine, took a genuine interest in our endeavor and, with his excellent customer service skills, made a real difference in our preparation phase. He patiently answered many questions, some of which had nothing to do with purchases of equipment or apparel at his store. He took the time to explain what touring was like and made positive adjustments to the bicycle.

Wayne Boroughs from thetouringstore.com patiently explained in depth the design and functionality of the Ortlieb panniers. He also described how to determine the capacity to purchase.

The novelty of our adventure universally elicited earnest support. A successful bicycle tour is dependent upon input from others with more expertise and experience. Thanks to all who made our trip so enjoyable.

Learn the story behind the book you've read.

Two Are Better

Midlife Newlyweds Bicycle Coast to Coast
By Tim and Debbie Bishop

After fifty-two years of life, Tim and Debbie Bishop finally found in each other that special someone they'd been searching for years to marry. In only ten weeks, they moved from marriage proposal and wedding, to Tim's "retirement" and relocation, to embarking on a cycling adventure of a lifetime. *Two Are Better* captures the joy and excitement of their odyssey.

Two Are Better: Midlife Newlyweds Bicycle Coast to Coast is a full-color, 208-page, 6" x 9" paperback book published by Open Road Press, including over 100 color photos of the Bishops' trip across the country. Learn the inspiring story, be challenged to make your own dreams come true, and enjoy a vicarious adventure across a beautiful land.

Also available in e-book formats.

Available online or through a bookseller near you

Wait until you see what's in

Wheels of Wisdom
Life Lessons for the Restless Spirit
By Tim and Debbie Bishop

Recognized eight times in book award contests

First place in:
- Inspiration
- Devotional
- Christian Nonfiction
- Christian Inspirational

Looking for more out of life?

After three tours totaling over 10,000 miles, Tim and Debbie Bishop have discovered wisdom and truth from the seat of a bicycle. In *Wheels of Wisdom*, the authors share the life lessons they learned on the open road.

When you're looking for enlightenment, you can find it almost anywhere, be it from watching two herons saunter across a Florida road, pedaling to a dead-end in a Kentucky tobacco field, or observing eagles flying overhead in Montana. In each lesson of this book, you'll find practical insights, inspiration, and encouragement—along with personal reflection questions that will help you:

- Adopt the right mind-set
- Conquer fear, worry, and inaction
- Overcome obstacles
- Relish life's journey

Certain principles are universal whether you are bicycling across America or chasing your own lifelong dream.

You may be continuing your education, connecting with new people, looking to change jobs, or simply wondering about your future. Wherever you are in life, *Wheels of Wisdom* will give you a fresh perspective and new motivation for your own adventure. Not only will you encounter meaningful truth as you travel vicariously to new places and meet new people, you'll also experience some genuine "God moments" and have some fun on the way.

So, pack up your dreams and passions and come along for the ride. It's time to learn on the open road!

You'll find *Wheels of Wisdom: Life Lessons for the Restless Spirit* online or at a bookseller near you.

Available online or through a bookseller near you

Wheels of Wisdom Accolades

PW	"A road map for life . . . incorporates faith without unnecessary preaching." – *Publishers Weekly*
BB	Selected twice as a "Featured Deal" on Bookbub

Book Awards	Placement	Category	Contest
NIEA WINNER	Winner	Inspiration	National Indie Excellence Awards
Readers' Favorite	Gold medal	Devotional	Readers' Favorite Int'l Book Awards
Indie Book Awards	Winner	Christian Nonfiction	Next Generation Indie Book Awards
Best Book Awards Winner	Winner	Christian Inspirational	Best Book Awards
Illumination	Bronze medal	Devotional	Illumination Book Awards
2018 Semifinalist	Semifinalist (1 of 20)	Nonfiction	Kindle eBook Awards
Indie Book Awards	Finalist (1 of 5)	Inspirational Nonfiction	Next Generation Indie Book Awards
IP	Bronze medal	Adult NF Pers. E-book	Independent Publisher (IPPY) Awards

Metaphors in Motion

Wisdom from the Open Road

By Tim and Debbie Bishop

Metaphors in Motion will give you more of what's in *Wheels of Wisdom*. Most of the contributors on the *Wheels of Wisdom* project agreed that the early manuscript had too many lessons in it. However, no one could agree on which ones should go. "They're all good!" was the common refrain. So, eight lessons were pulled out to become *Metaphors in Motion*, not because they were substandard, but because some themes were similar to ones already contained in *Wheels of Wisdom*.

If you're considering reading *Wheels of Wisdom* but haven't yet, take *Metaphors in Motion* for a spin. If you've already read *Wheels of Wisdom* and are looking for some more wisdom, it's here for you in this e-book. This book is now available in print.

Order online at www.openroadpress.com

ABOUT OPEN ROAD PRESS

What you do get when you combine faith, life experience, second chances, and thousands of miles of self-supported bicycle touring throughout America?

Inspiration • Hope • Encouragement

Adventure • Fun • Entertainment

You also get uplifting books that share the journey and what it teaches the willing traveler, including an eight-time award winner. *Wheels of Wisdom: Life Lessons for the Restless Spirit* has won four first-place book awards—in Inspiration, Devotional, Christian Nonfiction, and Christian Inspirational. Publishers Weekly dubbed it "a road map for life."

Check out our books at openroadpress.com. Take up the challenge to make meaning and adventure vital parts of your daily life.

Open Road Press • Love and Life by Bicycle

Questions, comments, and feedback are always welcome at openroadpress.com. We will do our best to respond to all constructive comments and questions.

Life Got You Down?
Need Help?

If you're 13-29 years old, reach out now at www.thehopeline.com/gethelp/.

It may just save your life.

www.ingramcontent.com/pod-product-compliance
Lightning Source LLC
Chambersburg PA
CBHW052029290426
44112CB00014B/2436